KT-514-044

3rd edition

Volleyball

- Key Tech
- Equipmer
- Advice fo
- Rules of t

volleyballengland

putting volleyball @
the heart of your community

796.3

02115115

Volleyball

Produced in collaboration with
Volleyball England

STRODE'S COLLEGE
LIBRARY

Produced for A & C Black by

Monkey Puzzle Media Ltd
Gissings Farm, Fressingfield
Suffolk IP21 5SH

Published in 2006 by

A & C Black Publishers Ltd
38 Soho Square, London W1D 3HB
www.acblack.com

Third edition 2006

Copyright © 2006, 2000, 1994
Volleyball England

ISBN-10: 0 7136 7900 X
ISBN-13: 978 0 7136 7900 7

All rights reserved. No part of this publication may be
reproduced in any form or by any means – graphic,
electronic or mechanical, including photocopying,
recording, taping or information storage and retrieval
systems – without the prior permission in writing
of the publishers.

Volleyball England has asserted its right under the
Copyright, Designs and Patents Act, 1988, to be
identified as the author of this work.

A CIP record for this book is available from the
British Library.

Note: While every effort has been made to ensure
that the content of this book is as technically accurate
and as sound as possible, neither the author nor the
publisher can accept responsibility for any injury or
loss sustained as a result of the use of this material.

A & C Black uses paper produced with elemental
chlorine-free pulp, harvested from managed
sustainable forests.

Acknowledgements
Cover and inside design by James Winrow for
Monkey Puzzle Media Ltd.
Cover photograph courtesy of Empics.
All other photographs courtesy of the Fédération
Internationale de Volleyball (FIVB).
Illustrations by Dave Saunders.

KNOW THE GAME is a registered trademark.

Printed and bound in China by C&C Offset Printing
Co. Ltd.

Note: Throughout the book players and officials are
referred to as 'he'. This should, of course, be taken
to mean 'he or she' where appropriate. Similarly, all
instructions are geared towards right-handed players
– left-handers should simply reverse these instructions.

CONTENTS

FOREWORD

Several hundred thousand copies of *Know The Game: Volleyball* have been sold since I wrote the first edition in 1958. For 50 years now my original policy has continued – all royalties from this book go to the National Volleyball Association, to promote the game further. I am glad that this policy continues into the new millennium.

When volleyball was first created in 1895, it was known as 'mintonette'; in Arab countries to this day it is called 'the flying ball'. I think 'the flying ball' is a delightful image for our game, which is now, with football and basketball, one of the world's top three recreational games. Volleyball is an Olympic sport, an indoor game, a beach game and a park game. For old and young, girls and boys, able-bodied and disabled, the skills and movements of the game make it a complete and inexpensive physical education.

This edition has been revised by Stephen Jones, Coach Education & Development Officer for Volleyball England. Knowing his understanding and passion for the game, and his grasp of the changes which creative games have to undergo, I can think of no one better qualified to help volleyball fly into the twenty-first century.

Don Anthony
Honorary Life President
Volleyball England

Large groups of spectators gather to watch an indoor volleyball match.

Beach volleyball is increasingly popular, and is one of the types of volleyball played at the Olympic Games.

INTRODUCTION

In 1895 William Morgan, P.E. Director at Holyoake YMCA gymnasium, invented a game in which an inflated bladder was 'batted' over a rope by two teams. Morgan wanted a simple sport which would be suitable for a variety of physical types, both fit and unfit, and which could be played almost anywhere. His new game was soon dubbed 'volleyball'.

The competition-standard game: six players per team, referees and – best of all – a big, cheering crowd.

A WORLD SPORT

Volleyball spread rapidly throughout the world: in 1947 the International Volleyball Federation (FIVB) was formed. In Tokyo in 1964 volleyball became the first Olympic team sport for both men and women. In 1996 beach volleyball made its debut at the Olympic Games in Atlanta. Sitting volleyball and standing volleyball for people with disabilities have each been part of the Paralympic Games since 1976.

CHARACTERISTICS OF THE GAME

Volleyball is played by two teams on a court divided by a net. There are different versions of the game available for specific circumstances. For example, adapted versions of the game for Key Stage 1 and 2 are 1v1 and 2v2 in primary school, Mini-Volleyball (3v3) for children, 2v2 beach volleyball, recreational 4v4 park volleyball and sitting volleyball for players with disabilities.

The object of volleyball is to send the ball over the net so that it hits the ground in the opponents' court, and to prevent the opponents doing the same. Each team is allowed three contacts to return the ball (in addition to a block contact – see page 16).

The ball is put into play with a service from behind the baseline, sending the ball over the net and into the opponents' court. The rally continues until the ball is grounded on the playing court, goes 'out', or a team fails to return it properly.

In both volleyball and beach volleyball the team winning a rally scores a point. This is known as rally point scoring. When the receiving team wins a rally it scores a point and the right to serve. Its players rotate one position clockwise.

Volleyball is now one of the most popular team games in the world, with an estimated one billion players worldwide.

VOLLEYBALL CONTESTS

World Championships at Senior, Junior and Youth levels for men and women take place every four years. The World League (men) and the World Grand Prix (women) are played annually by the world's top 12 national teams for a prize fund of over US$12 million. The five Continental Confederations hold their own championships every two years. The World Beach Grand Prix and World Beach Volleyball Championships are also part of the calendar of major volleyball events.

A player prepares to dig the ball.

FACILITIES AND EQUIPMENT

Organisers should ensure that the governing body's recommendations for the lay-out of the court (including its surrounds and the equipment used) are strictly adhered to, in order to provide a safe and secure environment in which to play.

THE COURT

The playing area is 18m long by 9m wide, surrounded by a 'free zone' of at least 3m. Indoors, the playing surface should be flat, non-slip, non-abrasive, dry and clean. Ideally it should be shock absorbing, to reduce injuries from repeated

jumping and landing on a non-yielding surface. Volleyball can also be played outdoors on sand or grass, which should be checked carefully for any sharp or dangerous objects.

▼ The standard court measurements.

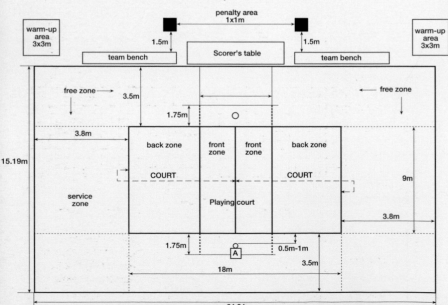

THE NET

The net is 2.43m high for men and 2.24m high for women. It is 1m deep and 9.5m long. It is essential that the net is taut, so that the ball will rebound from it.

Two flexible, vertical antennae are fastened to the net above the sidelines. The ball has to cross the net between the antennae.

THE POSTS

The posts must be rounded and smooth and be screwed to, or slotted into, the floor. They should have no dangerous or obstructing devices protruding from them. Freestanding posts or posts with weights are not permitted. Tie wires below head height should not be used to secure the posts. The posts must be between 0.5m and 1m from the outer edge of the court.

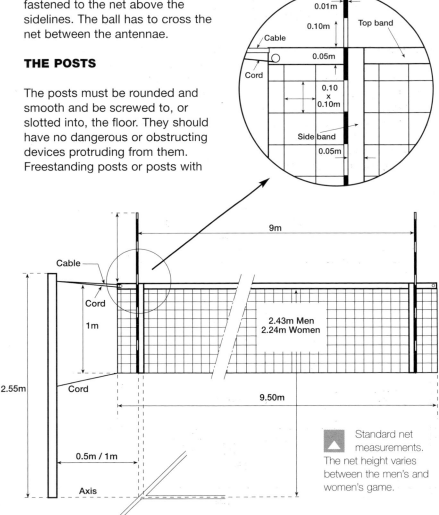

Standard net measurements. The net height varies between the men's and women's game.

A player using protective knee pads while retrieving the ball.

THE BALL

The ball is round, 65–67cm around, and weighs 260–280g. It is made with a flexible leather or synthetic leather case, inside which is a rubber bladder.

CLOTHING

Team members in volleyball competitions wear uniform, numbered shirts, shorts, and sports shoes. Shirts are numbered from 1 through to 18 only, and the numbers are 20cm high on the back, and 15cm high on the front.

In beach volleyball, players wear shorts and/or bathing suits. A jersey or tank top is allowed unless the tournament rules say otherwise, and players are allowed to wear a hat. Beach volleyball players play barefoot unless the referee has given them permission to wear shoes. Players are forbidden to wear any object that could cause injury, or give them an artificial advantage.

Competition players need to keep warm while they're not on the court, so will keep a tracksuit or something similar nearby for this purpose.

Volleyball is a highly dynamic game with lengthy rallies, particularly in the women's game. The volleyball kit should be comfortable (to allow for a full range of movement) and be cool during play. Most modern fabrics are soft and lightweight, providing superior moisture management during play.

Volleyball requires a lot of starting, stopping, and quick movements across and off the floor. Players' shoes should be designed with plenty of grip, and shock absorption for the jumping phase. It is essential that the shoe is designed to be light in weight, have good breathability, and be fast drying. This is normally achieved by a combination of leather, synthetic fabric weave and rubber to reinforce key areas of wear.

Protective kneepads will help you slide on the floor when attempting to retrieve a low ball on a hard court.

Players' clothing is light and comfortable to allow for huge jumps such as this!

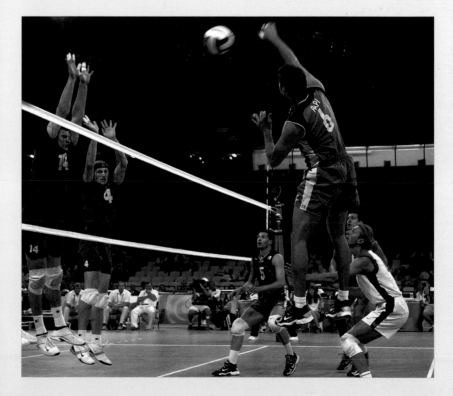

STARTING PLAY

There is a certain amount of formality at the start of a game of volleyball. The team captains and the referee for the day are usually introduced to each other. The captains then toss a coin for the right to decide who serves first.

CHOICE OF COURT

The two captains toss a coin: the winner can choose either to serve first or the court in which to start the match.

- After each set (see page 42), the teams change courts and the team that received service serves first in the following set.

- Before the beginning of the decisive set (the one that will decide the winner) a coin is tossed once more to decide the choice of court or service.

- In this last set, when one team has a total of eight points, the teams change courts; the team serving at the time of the change continues to serve.

PLAYER POSITIONS

At the moment the server hits the ball, all the other players must be standing on the court in their correct positions. These are shown in the diagram.

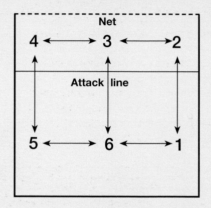

The three players who can play at the net are called front-row players and occupy positions 4 (front left), 3 (front centre) and 2 (front right). The other three are back-row players and occupy positions 5 (back left), 6 (back centre) and 1 (back right).

During service, the server (position 1 in the diagram) may move anywhere behind the baseline to serve.

At the moment the ball is served each front-row player must be nearer to the net than their corresponding back-row player, i.e. the player in position 4 must be in front of the player in position 5, 3 in front of 6 and 2 in front of 1. Also, each side player must be closer to their corresponding side line than is the middle player, i.e. 4 must be to the left of 3, 2 must be to the right of 3; and in the back row 5 must be to the left of 6 and 1 must be to the right of 6.

Once the ball has been served the players may move around and occupy any position on their court. However back-row players are not allowed to block or smash from in front of the attack line.

THE TEAMS

Each team consists of six players on court and a maximum of six substitutes (12 in total). If a team is reduced to less than six players, for example due to an injury or a sending-off, that team forfeits the match.

This player is about to serve to start play.

ROTATION OF PLAYERS

The same player carries on serving until their team loses a rally. When the receiving team wins a rally it wins the right to serve and its players rotate one position clockwise, i.e. the player in position 2 rotates to position 1 to serve; the player in position 1 rotates to position 6 etc., as shown in the diagram.

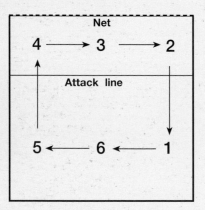

Player rotation before the team starts serving again. (Note that numbers 1 to 6 refer to the court positions, not to the numbers that appear on the players' shirts.)

BACK-ROW PLAYERS

The rules prevent back-row players from doing two things:

- They may not play the ball directly from within the attack area into the opponent's court, unless the ball is below the height of the net.
- They may not block.

A back-row player can smash the ball, providing the take-off for the smash is clearly behind the attack line. The back-row smasher can land in the attack area.

> The starting players and rotation order of a team can be changed before the beginning of each set. The change must be noted on the scoresheet.

A player attempting a spike.

Volleyball players must develop the skills to hit the ball with speed, power and accuracy.

THE GAME IN ACTION

Volleyball relies on the accuracy and pace of the serve to apply pressure to the opposition. The opposition's job is to absorb this pressure, then build up an attack using three contacts on the ball, to swing the pressure back on the serving team.

A player retrieves the ball on one arm under pressure.

THREE TOUCHES

The player in position 1 starts play with a service. The team receiving the service is allowed a maximum of three contacts to return the ball to the serving team's side of the net. No more than three contacts are allowed. (An attempted block does not count as one of a team's three contacts.)

Players are not allowed to contact the ball twice in succession (unless one of the contacts is an attempted block).

The normal sequence of play is as follows:

- The receiving team attempts to direct the serve or attack towards the net.

- A specialised player, the 'setter', is positioned at the net: the setter fields the ball high and close to the net.

- An attack player, the 'smasher', jumps to hit the ball down into the opponents' court.

The new receiving team attempts to block this attack at the net, or to 'dig' the ball, usually in the back court. A successful block sends the ball back into the opposition court, where they get another three contacts to set up a counterattack. If the serving team digs the ball they have two more contacts, a 'set' and a 'smash', to make an attack.

HANDLING THE BALL

Volleyball's handling rules are:

- The ball may be played with any part of the body.

- The ball must be hit, not caught and/or thrown.

- The ball may touch various parts of the body, provided that the contacts take place simultaneously.

There are two exceptions:

1. At the team's first hit (when receiving the serve or first attacking) the ball may contact various parts of the body consecutively, provided that the contacts occur during one action, i.e. a double touch is allowed.

2. When blocking, consecutive contacts may be made by one or more blockers, provided that the contacts occur during one action.

BALL IN AND BALL OUT

- The ball is 'in' when it touches inside and on the line of the court.
- The ball is 'out' when: the part of the ball that contacts the floor is completely outside the boundary lines; the ball hits an object outside the court, e.g. the ceiling; or the ball touches the posts, antennae, or net outside the sidebands.

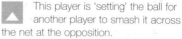
This player is 'setting' the ball for another player to smash it across the net at the opposition.

THE SERVICE

The service is the act of putting the ball into play by the right-hand back-row player (position 1). The server is not allowed to strike a ball resting on their other hand. The ball must be tossed in the air or released before being served. The ball must be hit with one hand or part of the arm.

At the moment of service the server must be standing in the service zone behind the baseline. If using a jump serve, the server must take off from behind the baseline. It is a fault if the server touches the baseline before striking the ball. After the service the player may step on to or land in the court.

The server is not allowed a second attempt at serving, even if the ball is allowed to bounce on the floor after the initial toss.

SIMULTANEOUS CONTACTS AND DOUBLE FAULTS

- If two opponents simultaneously touch the ball above the net, the player from the team on whose side the ball does not fall is deemed to have touched it last. The other team then has three touches of the ball.
- If, after a simultaneous touch, the ball falls on to the court, the team on whose side the ball falls loses the rally. If the ball falls outside the court, the team on the other side of the net loses the rally.
- If two players on the same team play the ball and touch it at the same time, it counts as two touches (except in the case of a block, where it only counts as one).
- If faults are committed by opponents at exactly the same time, a 'double fault' is called and the rally is replayed.

Two players leap up to block the ball. Even if these two players touch the ball while blocking it, the block is legal as long as they make contact with the ball at the same moment.

GOOD V BAD SERVES

The service is considered good if the ball passes:

- over the net into the opponents' court, and
- between the two vertical antennae marking the width of the net.

The service is a fault if the ball:

- passes over or outside the antennae above the net
- touches a player or object (other than the net) before going into the opponents' court
- goes under the net
- falls outside the limits of the court.

If the serve is faulty, the referee indicates 'side-out', and the opponents win a point and gain service.

A served ball that touches the net and passes over to the opposite side remains in play.

A good service is a crucial part of any team's game.

NET PLAY AND FAULTS

If the ball touches the net during play and passes into the opponents' court, it is not a fault (this includes service). Even if the ball goes into the net and rebounds back, it can then still be played by any player other than the last one to touch it, providing the maximum three touches are not exceeded.

Contact with the net

- If the force of the ball hitting the net causes the net to come into contact with an opposing player, this does not constitute a fault on the part of the latter (see below).

- It is a fault if a player touches the net when playing the ball.

- If two players from opposing teams simultaneously touch the net, this is known as a 'double fault', and the point is replayed.

- It is not a fault for a player to touch the posts.

Playing the ball above the net

When blocking, a player may play the ball when it is still on the other side of the net, as long as he or she does not interfere with the opponents' play before or during the latter's attack hit. It is a fault to play the ball on the other side of the net before the opponents have finished their attack.

Players are allowed to pass their hands beyond the net after an attack hit, provided that the ball contact was made on their side of the net. It is a fault for a player to reach over the net to attack the ball, or to touch the net on the follow-through from the smashing action.

Contact under the net

Players are permitted to touch the opponents' court with a foot or feet, hand or hands, as long as some part of the foot or hand remains in contact with, or directly above, the centre line.

It is a fault if any other part of a player's body contacts the opponents' court.

> **SPATIAL AWARENESS**
>
> Spatial awareness is the ability to work within one's own space and to organise objects in relation to one's own body. It is an essential quality for a volleyball player to develop, particularly around the net during play.

A defender leaps slightly too late to make the block.

SUBSTITUTIONS

Each team is allowed a maximum of six substitutions per set. A player who starts a set and is then substituted is allowed to re-enter the game, but only for the player he or she originally replaced. Neither the starting player nor substitute can be substituted again in that set. If a team becomes incomplete through injury to one of its players, and if all other substitutions have been used, a substitute can replace the injured player even if he or she has already played in another position. This is called an 'exceptional substitution'.

Coach talking to players during a time-out. Coaches use time-outs to give their team tactical advice.

TIME-OUTS

- Each team is allowed to call two 'time-outs' in each set, to get advice from their coach.
- The players leave the court and go to the free zone near their team bench.
- Each time-out lasts 30 seconds.

'LIBERO' PLAYER

The 'libero' is a specialised defensive player who is used to improve the back-court defence and reception. The libero enhances the defensive aspects of the game and is selected for strong back-court defence skills and service-receive skills. The libero is often used to replace taller, less agile players in back court.

The libero's play is controlled by certain rules:

- He or she is not allowed to serve, complete an attack hit (i.e. hit the ball above the height of the net) from anywhere on court, or to block.

- Another player may not complete an attack hit if the ball has been volleyed by a libero in the front zone.

- The libero is, however, allowed to set up an attack from behind the attack line.

- The libero can be substituted for a player in the back row, provided that the ball is dead and the whistle for service has not been blown.

- Liberos wear a shirt of a different colour from their team-mates.

Each team is free to use a libero or not. The libero is allowed to enter and leave the court at any side-out opportunity to replace any back-court player without a substitution taking place. The advantage is in replacing a taller player who has weaknesses in defence throughout the game, without using up substitutions.

Only the team captain or coach can request substitutions, and then only when the ball is dead.

The libero player passes the ball from the back court towards the setter. Libero players are specialists who are brought on for their service reception and defensive skills.

FUNDAMENTALS

Volleyball players need to be able to move about so they can observe the flight of the ball, analyse the movements of players through the net, and contact the ball accurately. These 'fundamental' movements are essential qualities of a player during the game.

BASIC SKILLS

There are a number of basic mental and movement skills that underpin all the individual and team skills in volleyball. They are known as the 'fundamentals' and they recur sequentially during play.

The 'fundamentals cycle' is shown below. The four key stages are:

1. Ready for Action
2. Right Time, Right Place
3. Ball Control
4. Finish and Link.

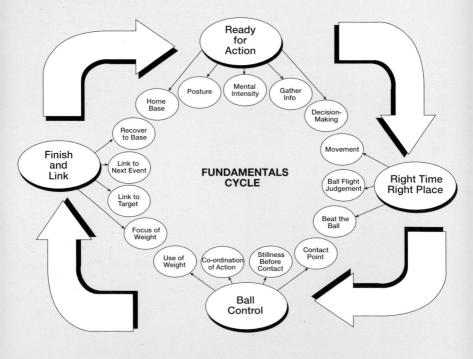

Ready for Action

Posture · Mental Intensity · Gather Info

Home Base

Decision-Making

Recover to Base

Movement

Finish and Link

Link to Next Event

FUNDAMENTALS CYCLE

Ball Flight Judgement

Right Time Right Place

Link to Target

Beat the Ball

Focus of Weight

Use of Weight · Co-ordination of Action · Stillness Before Contact · Contact Point

Ball Control

These players are mentally and physically ready for action, waiting to receive a serve.

It is easiest to understand what each of these stages means by describing what players do during a particular action, for example, when they are receiving a serve.

1. READY FOR ACTION

These are the key steps players take in order to be 'ready for action':

- **Home-base position**
  Where do I stand on court in order to be in the best position to cover all of the area that is my responsibility?
  Where do I stand in relation to my team-mates?

- **Posture**
  Am I ready physically to move quickly to get to the ball: feet shoulder width apart, knees slightly bent, balanced?

- **Mental intensity**
  Am I focused and concentrating?

- **Gather information**
  What type of serve is the server going to use? In which direction is the server likely to serve?

- **Decision-making**
  Where is the ball going?
  Do I play it or do I leave it?
  Do I use a volley or a forearm pass to receive the ball?

> **The most effective volleyball players are usually very good at tracking the ball in flight and predicting where it will land, while preparing the correct technique to apply to the ball.**

Having played the ball, this player immediately needs either to join the attack or defence. Once the ball has gone over the net, he must quickly recover his base position.

2. RIGHT TIME, RIGHT PLACE

These are the key considerations for players when deciding whether they are in the right place at the right time:

- **Ball-flight judgment**
  Accurately read the flight of the ball, and anticipate the position to which I have to move so that I can play the ball with control.

- **Movement**
  Move to play the ball using the correct footwork, or move to support the receiving player, or move to prepare to attack. Keep hips and eyes level as I move.

- **Beat the ball**
  Time my movement so that I get to the contact position before the ball arrives.

3. BALL CONTROL

These are the key elements for players to consider when they actually play the ball:

- **Contact point**
  Has to be behind the ball, to contact it between the waist and knees with arms about 45 degrees to the floor.

- **Stillness before contact**
  Be balanced before contact. Mentally focus on the target to which the ball must be passed.

- **Co-ordination of action**
  Use of legs, hips and arms in the right sequence.

- **Use of weight**
  Control the speed and trajectory of the ball by transferring whole body weight in the direction of the target. Don't swing my arms.

4. FINISH AND LINK

This is the final sequence for players in action on court:

- **Focus of weight**
  I need to focus weight where my arms contact the ball.

- **Link to target**
  I must finish action/movement in the correct direction (follow-through).
  I must see the ball going to the target in my mind's eye.

- **Link to next event**
  Having passed the ball to the setter, I must move to attack or move to cover the smasher.

- **Recover to base**
  The ball has gone over the net: I must move to the defensive base position to get ready to defend against the opponent's attack.

▲ A good player remains focused on the ball right through to finish and link.

▼ Players need to be ready for action at every moment the ball is in play.

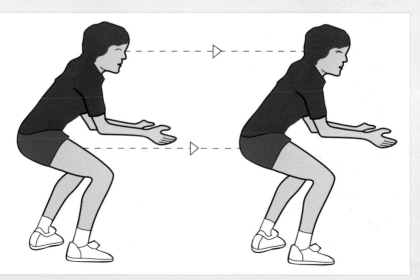

SKILLS

There are five basic skills that are required to play the game effectively: the serve, dig, volley, smash and block. More complex skills, such as diving and rolling, are used in extreme retrieves of the ball.

SERVICE

The serve is used to start every rally. It is the only move in volleyball in which the player has complete control. Every player should develop a serve that is low risk so that they can be certain of getting the ball into court (this will be an underarm serve). Players should also work on a serve that can be used to put pressure on the opposition – a ball that is accurately placed or is travelling quickly.

There are three main serves used, two of which are described here.

Underarm serve

1. The left toe points at the target (for right-handers).
2. Weight is on the back foot.
3. Ball is dropped as striking arm comes through.
4. The arm moves in a straight line. Weight moves forward.
5. Arm and body weight move towards target.

▼ The service action should be smooth throughout.

Overarm serve

Start by standing with feet shoulder-width apart, left foot facing the target and right foot behind and to the side of the left foot. Your knees should be slightly flexed.

1. Hold the ball out in front with the left hand at shoulder height.

2. Toss the ball with the left hand and at the same time draw the hitting hand and arm back with the elbow high.

3. Transfer the weight from the right foot to the left foot and propel the hand through.

4. Contact the ball with the palm of the hand.

▼ Players can get more power on the ball with an overarm serve.

The jump serve is an advanced serve, used by players to generate speed and power.

PROBING THE OPPOSITION

Serving can be used tactically to highlight weaknesses in the opposition's reception skills, or apply more pressure on the basic skills. For example, by serving at one of the opposition's major attackers you may be able to disrupt their approach pattern and weaken their smash.

THE 'DIG'

The forearm pass, often called the 'dig', is used to play a ball that is travelling too fast and low to volley. It is used most often to receive the serve or an attacking shot from the opponents.

The player should move behind the ball and, when it is in front of them, play it between waist and ankle height, and between the legs. The forearms are brought together to form a platform from which the ball rebounds.

 The 'dig': 1) Assume a 'ready to play' stance.
2) Move in line with the ball flight.
3) 'Bump' the ball – don't hit it. Follow to target.

▼ The forearm pass, or 'dig', in action.

VOLLEYING TO THE OPPOSITION

Sometimes a team is forced to volley the ball over the net on the third touch. If this happens, the ball should be played as low and as flat as possible into a space between two players, thus making it more difficult for the opposition to control the ball.

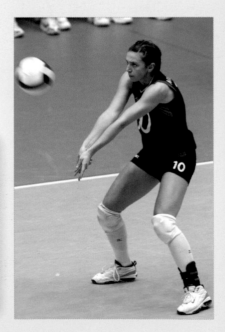

THE VOLLEY

The volley is a two-handed pass that is played when the ball is above the forehead. Once mastered it is the most accurate method of passing the ball.

The volley is most commonly used to set up an attack. The ball is played high, and comes down about 1m back from the net, so that an attacker can jump and smash it down on to the opponents' court. This is called 'setting' the ball, and the player who sets is called the 'setter'.

The setter is a key person in the team, controlling and directing the attack rather like the quarterback in American football. He or she has the option of setting the ball 'high', 'medium' or 'quick', and to attackers approaching from the front or behind. Teams usually play with one or two specialist setters. The volley is also used to receive a slow-moving ball from the opposition (called a 'free ball') and pass it to the setter at the net.

▼ The volley: 1) Assume a 'ready to play' stance.
2) Watch the ball.
3) Be ready to play the ball, on your mid-body line and above your hairline. Bend the knees and face the direction in which you wish to play the ball.
4) Touch the ball.
5) Move your body weight through in the direction of the ball and extend your arms.

In the volley, the ball should be played 'quietly' with relaxed arms, wrists and fingers.

THE SMASH

The 'smash', otherwise known as the 'spike', is the main attack shot used in volleyball. The smasher runs in and jumps with both feet close to the net (about 1m away), then strikes the ball with one hand down into the opponents' court. Variations that the smasher may use include:

- smashing a high set diagonally across court or down the line.

- smashing a quick set – the attacker jumps at the same time as the setter sets the ball.

- hitting the ball off the block and out of court.

- hitting a controlled, slower smash (off-speed smash) accurately into a space.

- tipping the ball just over the top of the block into the space behind it (similar to a drop shot in tennis).

▼ The smash: 1) Run in towards the net.
2) Swing your arms back.
3) Jump off both feet, bringing your arms forward.
4) Lead with the non-hitting hand, and bring the hitting hand back.
5) Strike the ball, being careful not to hit the net on your follow-through.
6) Control the landing on two feet with no forward travel.

 Ball being smashed.

At a higher level of play, teams normally have two or three smashers approaching the net from different positions and at different times. The setter decides which player is best to set the ball to. These multiple attack options make it more difficult for the defending team to position its block and defence.

When smashing, the ball must be contacted in front of the hitting shoulder. This provides greater power and allows you to observe the movements of the opposition's block.

THE BLOCK

The block is the first line of defence against the smash. It may be performed by one, two or three front-row players, who jump and reach across the net with their hands to deflect the smashed ball back into the opponents' court.

Players leaping to block an opponent's attack.

The block can also stop the smasher from targeting a particular area of the court, thus channelling the ball to where the back-court defenders have been placed.

The block: 1) Stand about half a metre from the net, with your elbows forward, hands in front of shoulders and knees slightly bent.
2) Side step into position, to where you think the ball will be smashed over the net.
3) Time your jump to match the jump of the opposition's smasher.
4) Reach up and over the net to block the ball. Spread your fingers.

A two-person block is the most common in volleyball. This is because it is the best compromise between strong blocking and adequate court defence. It is too easy to smash past a single blocker, and if a triple block is used there is too much court for the remaining three, non-blocking defenders to cover.

When using the sprawl technique, make sure your hand is in contact with the floor. This will allow the ball to bounce off the back of your hand effectively.

FLOOR DEFENCE

The block is the first line of defence in volleyball. Floor defence is the second line of defence. If the ball gets past the block, the defenders must try to keep the ball off the floor. If possible, they must also pass the ball to the setter, so that a

▼ A desperate defensive dive. With the ball this far away, all the defender can do is hope to keep it in the air.

counterattack can be set up. If the defender has anticipated correctly and moved to the spot where the ball has been hit, he or she will then be able to stay on their feet and use either an underhand dig or an overhand defence shot. On some occasions, however, the player will have to use a sprawl or dive to get to the ball.

TACTICAL AWARENESS

A volleyball rally follows a cyclical pattern of play, continually changing between attack and defence. It is not enough to know how to execute the fundamentals and skills of the game. Players must be able to move from one phase of the game to the next and know how to recognise the cues that help them to make the right decisions about what to do next.

TEAM TACTICS

The sequence of diagrams on these pages show how a team might organise itself as it moves through the phases of a typical volleyball rally. A key feature of successful teams is their ability to move smoothly from one phase to the next, for example from attack and cover, to defensive positions, to block and floor defence.

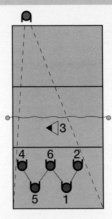

Service reception positions when defending.

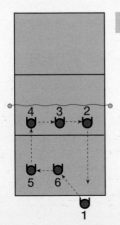

Rotation after service.

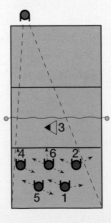

Possible movement in service reception.

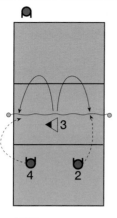

Setting up an attack (player 3 volleys the ball, player 2 or 4 smashes it).

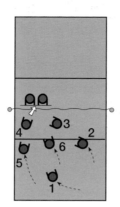

Covering or backing up the attack after player 4 has smashed the ball.

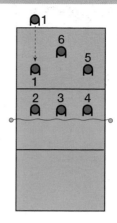

Establishing a defensive base when serving.

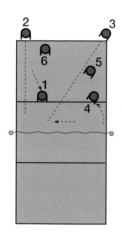

Blocking and floor defence.

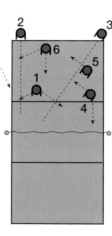

Possible movement in defence.

It is easier to move forwards to play the ball, so aim to pass the ball slightly in front of your team-mate.

SCORING

The team winning a rally scores a point and gets the right to serve. Official matches are played to the best of five sets for both men and women.

WINNING SETS

In the first four sets the set is won by the first team to reach 25 points, with a two-point advantage, e.g. 25–23, 26–24, 35–33. If the score is 2 sets each at the end of the fourth set, the match goes to a tie-break. A fifth, tie-break set is played to 15 points. As in all the other sets, a two-point advantage is needed to win, e.g. 15–13, 16–14, 22–20.

The International Rulebook and Official Scoresheet are available from Volleyball England (www.volleyballengland. org)

VARIATIONS

Some competitions, especially those for young players, are to the best of three sets. In local tournaments matches often have a time limit, e.g. best of three sets, each set a maximum of 15 minutes.

Beach volleyball is scored differently – see page 44 for an explanation.

 A different perspective on the volleyball game.

Everyone – players, coaches and officials – has a duty to make each volleyball match run as smoothly as possible, and to follow the rules of the game.

PLAYERS

Players must know and abide by the rules. They must accept the referees' decisions without disputing them.

COACHES

The team coach can either sit on the team bench nearest to the scorer's table or stand or walk within the free zone in front of the bench. The coach is allowed to give instructions to the players during the match.

The coach can call time-outs and substitutions. If a team does not have a coach, the team captain assumes all the coach's duties.

> **During the game only the team's captain is allowed to speak to the officials.**

Players must not protest the referee's decision.

OFFICIALS AND SANCTIONS

In official competitions a first referee, second referee, scorer and four line judges are required. A team of ball retrievers is sometimes used to minimise delays between rallies, making sure a ball is always ready for the server at each end. At a lower level, one referee and a scorer are often adequate.

THE FIRST REFEREE

The first referee is in overall control of the match and his or her decisions are final. The first referee is positioned on a stand above one end of the net. The referee whistles for service and to signal the end of each rally, indicating the fault or action that ended the rally and which team has the next service. The first referee is responsible for calling serving faults, and judging ball handling and faults at the top of the net. The first referee is also responsible for disciplining any inappropriate behaviour and may act on the advice of the other officials.

▼ The elevated position of the first referee puts them in an ideal place to police the play at the top of the net.

THE SECOND REFEREE

The second referee stands on the floor, off the court, opposite the first referee. He or she is responsible for checking that the teams rotate their order correctly, calling faults at the bottom of the net and centre line, and controlling time-outs and substitutions. The second referee must also check that back-row players do not move forward to block or attack from inside the attack line.

Officials: 1) Scorer
2) Second Referee
3) Team Bench
4) Line Judge
5) First Referee
The first referee's view must be approximately 0.5m above the level of the net.

SANCTIONS

1. 'Verbal warning': minor offence (time wasting, showing dissent). No penalty to player or team.
2. 'Yellow card': second minor offence/first severe offence (rudeness to the referee). Player's team loses rally (a point is given to the opposition).
3. 'Red card': offensive conduct towards officials or opponents. Player sent off for remainder of set. A legal substitution may be used if available. Otherwise, the team is incomplete and loses the set.
4. 'Red and yellow cards': Aggressive conduct, threat of aggression. Player sent off for remainder of match.

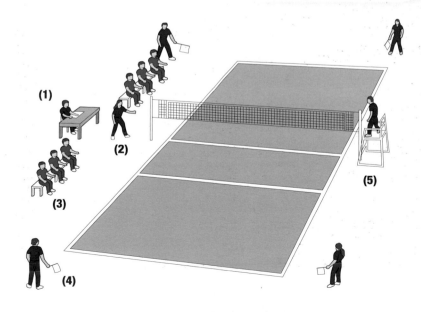

(1)
(2)
(3)
(4)
(5)

THE SCORER

The scorer sits at a table behind the second referee and completes the scoresheet by recording team lists, the rotational order of each team in each set, points scored, time-outs, substitutions and any cards given by the first referee.

THE LINE JUDGES

Two or four line judges can be used and they make decisions on ball in and ball out. They also indicate to the first referee if the server has committed a foot fault, if the ball touches the block before landing out of court, and if the ball crosses the net outside the antennae. Each line judge has a flag.

HAND SIGNALS

The officials do not usually speak to the players; they communicate their decisions using a whistle and hand signals. Only the team captain is allowed to speak to the referee and then only to ask for an explanation of the decision given. The most common signals used by the first and second referee and line judges are shown on this page and opposite.

Double contact

Ball out

Reaching beyond the net

Net touched by a player

Double fault

Blocking fault or screening

Misconduct

Crossing the centre line/ball underneath net

Service authorisation

Team delay

Ball touched

Substitution

Back-court attack hit

Ball held

End of set

Delay in service

Four contacts

Positional fault

Indicates team to
serve next

Ball in

Time-out

Change court

43

BEACH VOLLEYBALL

Beach volleyball is played on a slightly smaller court (16m x 8m) than volleyball but with the same net heights (2.43m for men, 2.24m for women). International competitions are played with teams of two players. No substitutes are allowed.

SCORING AND MATCHES

Rally point scoring has been introduced into beach volleyball to bring it into line with the indoor game. Each time a team wins a rally it gains a point.

Matches are usually the best of three sets – up to 21 points in the first two and up to 15 in the third, deciding, set. If the score reaches 14–14 play is continued until one of the teams has a two-point lead (i.e. 16–14, 17–15).

When choosing which end to start from, remember that the direction of the wind or position of the sun will affect the game.

OTHER DIFFERENCES

Aside from the scoring, there are several other key differences. In beach volleyball:

- there are no centre line or attack lines on the court
- players can go 'under the net' provided they do not interfere with their opponents
- a block counts as one of a team's three hits
- if a player volleys the ball over the net it must be played in a direction at right angles to the player's shoulders
- teams switch ends after every five points
- each team is allowed one time-out per set
- no coaching is allowed during the match
- the ball is softer – inflated to 0.175–0.225kg/cm^2 (0.3–0.325kg/cm^2 indoors)
- the ball is also slightly larger – 66–68cm circumference (65–67cm indoors).

...DRMS OF VOLLEYBALL

**traditional volleyball and beach volleyball,
other variations on the game, intended to
appeal to a wider audience.**

...nal Volleyball
...s introduced a new
...ational volleyball, 'park
...is played outside.
...d FIVB rules state that
...s played between two
...r players each; the
...be single sex or mixed.
...smaller (14m x 7m) and
...43m high for men, 2.3m
...nd 2.24m for women.
...scoring is used, with
...to score when they are
...e service. Each set is
...25 points, with a two-point
...required to win the set.
...can be one, two or three
...reed by the teams. However,
...olley is designed to promote
...nal volleyball, the rules can
...ded with agreement to suit
...s and conditions.

A player gets low to dig the ball
out of the sand.

VOLLEYBALL FOR ALL AGES

Volleyball can be played in many
different game formats – 1v1, 2v2,
3v3 or 4v4, for example. These are
often used as a way of introducing
the game to different age groups or
abilities. 'Let's Play Volleyball', the
Volleyball England Schools and
Clubs Developmental Model, uses
these formats to broaden the
understanding young players have
of the game:

- 1v1 is often used at Key Stage
  1 in primary schools as a way
  of introducing volleyball to
  young children.

- 2v2 encourages more
  teamwork at Key Stage 2.

- This is developed into 3v3
  (Mini-Volleyball) and 4v4 (Super
  Mini-Volleyball) at Key Stage 3
  and 4 in upper school.

The simplicity and nature of the
game is good for teams with any
number of players to play in parks
or on beaches up and down the
country. Volleyball can be played
by mixed groups of different ages
and genders.

Beach volleyball can be brought into city centres, using
iconic locations as backdrops. Matches at the 2012 Olympic
Games will be played on London's Horseguards Parade.

Beach volleyball is extremely popular – spectator numbers at major events grew from 60,000 in 1989 to 463,000 ten years later.

OLYMPIC SPORT

Beach volleyball was introduced into the Olympic Games at Atlanta, USA in 1996. Since then it has grown in popularity worldwide, and especially throughout the UK. Britain has had its greatest successes in the beach version of the game, with a women's team finishing 9th in Atlanta. The best players have in the main come from USA, Brazil and Australia. Unlimited access to good weather and beaches gives players from these countries a big advantage.

TACTICS

While many of the techniques are similar, the tactical side of the game is very different. Teams of two players use a smaller court and a slightly heavier ball, made up of brightly coloured panels. Each player often fulfils a different role on the court:

- Taller players provide a specialist blocking role.
- More agile players may be best placed on the back court, in a more defensive role.

Blocking positions on the net are predetermined by the player at the net, who signals covertly behind his or her back to the other player. The defensive player behind will usually line up cross court or down the line.

SERVING

The jump serve dominates beach volleyball, largely due to the power that is generated in the approach. Weather can play a critical factor in the type of serve used, with many players preferring a topspin or 'float' serve for reliability during adverse conditions. When the sun is directly overhead, the 'sky' or 'moon' ball, a serve high into the sky using an underarm movement, can make opponents look directly into the sun and cause them difficulty. This serve is also often used in windy conditions as the ball moves erratically when descending.

OVERHAND DIG

The major difference between the beach and indoor version of the game is the 'overhand dig', performed with flat, closed hands, one on top of each other, or with a closed hand (called a 'tomahawk') using the same grip position as an underhand dig, but overhead. The technique is best used when the ball is being lobbed directly over your head as it allows the player to put more movement through the ball with the chopping motion.

SPIKE ATTACK

The spike attack differs from indoors only by the speed of the hitting action. Winning points on the beach does not have to be done with the strongest of attacks but through good placement. It is normal for the attacker to look at the defenders' position and hit the ball away from them. Better beach players usually manage to have at least 3–4 looks at their opponents before execution of the shot.

OTHER F

As well a
there a
broaden its

PARK VOLL

The Internatio
Federation h
form of recre
volley', whic
The codifi
park volley
teams of fo
teams may
The court i
the net is
for mixed
Rally poin
teams ab
receiving
played to
advantag
Matches
sets as a
as park
recreatio
be ame
the tea

Retrieving the
with a dig pass.

SITTING VOLLEYBALL

The main differences between traditional volleyball and sitting volleyball are:

- The court is smaller at 10m x 6m, and the net is lower at 1.15m for men and 1.05m for women.

- Some part of a player's body from the buttocks to the shoulders must remain in contact with the floor.

- The serve can be blocked.

- A player's position on court is judged by the buttocks, so it is permissible for the feet or legs to touch the baseline on service, or to go over the centre line, for example.

Only players with physical disabilities can play in international sitting volleyball matches. Club-level sitting volleyball is played by integrated teams of disabled and able-bodied athletes.

In all forms of volleyball, players must have quick reactions to the movement of play.

STARTING OUT

Volleyball is a simple game that does not require any expensive equipment. It is suitable for all ages, from eight-year-olds to 'young-at-heart' pensioners. It's never too late and almost never too early in life to give volleyball a try.

SMALL-SIDED GAMES

When starting to play, or when first introducing the game, do not play six-a-side immediately; instead play small-sided games, for example 3v3 or 4v4 on a smaller court. That way everyone gets more opportunity to play the ball and learn the skills more quickly.

PLAYING IN COMPETITIONS

The simplest form of volleyball, played over a washing line in the garden with a soft ball, is a far cry from the organised indoor game with 12 players on the court. Volleyball England encourages clubs to forge links with the community and local schools, providing more opportunities to play.

The 'Let's Play Volleyball' programme includes a number of initiatives to make this happen. The programme includes the Volley 1-2-3 Club Accreditation Scheme, which encourages clubs to provide junior development, coaching schemes and school links through the local School Sports Co-ordination Scheme.

Anyone interested in initiatives to get people into volleyball should visit the Volleyball England website at www.volleyballengland.org.

ADAPTED RULES

- Up to and including 4v4 the ball may only be contacted on or above the knee.
- A 'fast-catch' volley is allowed in under-10 (U10), under-11 (U11) and in local beginner-level under-12 (U12) competition.
- Girls may play in a boys' team up to and including U14 age group competition.

Spectators can expect to see acrobatic leaps such as this in competition.

COURT SIZES

Court dimensions for age groups are shown below. Many venues have badminton and netball lines, in which case alternative dimensions can also be used.

U12 12m x 5m or use badminton court inner lines (11.88m x 5.18m).

U13 12m x 6m or use badminton court inner back lines and outer sidelines (11.88m x 6.1m).

U14 14m x 7m or use badminton court outer backlines and outer sidelines (13.44m x 6.1m).

U15 16m x 9m or for inexperienced players at a local level, 'Short Court 6' on a 16m x 9m court. This can be achieved by putting a net along the long axis of a netball court (30.5m x 15.25m) to give up to three volleyball courts 15.25m long x 9m wide. At least one sideline on each court needs to be marked.

TEACHING GUIDELINES

Here are some guidelines to help coaches and teachers make learning volleyball fun and successful:

- **Lightweight balls**
  Beginners should use lightweight teaching volleyballs or foam balls – neither of these will hurt their hands. Do not use soccer balls, netballs or moulded rubber balls.

- **Make do without a net**
  If a volleyball net is not available, use a rope with coloured braids attached as court dividers.

- **Net positioning**
  Position the net lengthways, down the centre of the sports hall. This provides space for a number of smaller courts rather than only one large court. Many small-sided games give more ball contacts and playing opportunity than one six-sided game.

- **Net height**
  The net or rope should be higher than the reach height of the tallest child. This ensures that attack shots have to be high, which gives the defenders more time to react to the ball. This helps rallies become longer, which is more fun.

- **Add competition**
  Introduce competitive games right from the start. Allowing weaker players to catch and throw the ball in 1v1 and 2v2 games, while they are gradually learning the volley skills, means everyone can have fun right from the start.

- **Add tactics**
  Emphasise the use of basic tactics from the beginning, for example attacking from near the net; moving back early to defend your court; or attacking to an empty space.

- **Go easy**
  Rules should be introduced gradually and when appropriate. Don't be too strict, especially on handling, at the outset.

- **Be adaptable**
  Make up special rules to help achieve the learning aims, e.g. there must be at least two touches before a team can return the ball over the net, which will improve passing skills.

- **Let them play**
  In the early stages, don't stop games too often to correct errors. Instead, work with individuals to improve their personal skills.

Brazil celebrate a win against Russia in the World Grand Prix 2006.

- **Be encouraging**
  Provide practices and drills at which the beginner can be successful.

- **Discourage specialisation**
  It is essential that every player should learn the fundamentals of all the positions (setter, smasher, etc.), so that they appreciate the demands of each role. Don't let players specialise too early.

The Mini-Volleyball and the Podium Butterfly ball are 'soft touch' balls, which are good for beginners.

VOLLEYBALL CHRONOLOGY

1896 After a demonstration given at the YMCA in Springfield, USA, the name 'Mintonette' is replaced with 'Volleyball'.

1900 The rules as modified by W.E. Day are accepted and published by the YMCA.

1910 By this time volleyball has reached Canada, Cuba, Japan, China and the Philippines.

1914 George Fisher, secretary of the YMCA War Office, includes volleyball in the recreation and education programme for the American armed forces.

1915 In Europe, volleyball arrives on the French beaches of Normandy and Brittany with American soldiers fighting in the First World War.

1919 During the First World War, Dr. George J. Fisher, as Secretary of the YMCA War Work Office, makes volleyball a part of the programme in military training camps, both in the USA and abroad.

1920 Players in the Philippines develop the first kind of spike. It is known as the Filipino bomb.

1922 The first national federation is founded in Czechoslovakia, quickly followed by Bulgaria. The first national championship is played in the USA, in which only YMCA teams compete.

1924 The programme for the Olympic Games in Paris includes a demonstration of 'American sports', and volleyball is among these.

1925 Volleyball is played for the first time in the Netherlands.

1927 The Japanese Volleyball Federation is founded.

1928 The US Volleyball Association is founded.

1933 The first national championship is held in the USSR, where there are already over 400,000 players. *Volleyball: Man's Game* by Robert E. Laveaga, and *Volleyball for Women* by Katherine M. Montgomery are published.

1935 Crosses are marked on the floor to determine player position. Touching the net is now considered a foul.

1938 The Czechs perfect blocking, which is officially introduced into the rules as 'a counteraction at the net by one or two adjacent players'.

1940 William G. Morgan, the creator of volleyball, dies at the age of 68.

1942 During the Second World War volleyball draws crowds among the troops, even aboard aircraft carriers. Volleyball is recommended by American Chiefs of Staff for training the troops as a sport to keep troops in condition, strengthen their morale, and teach them to work as a group.

1947 Egypt is the first Arab and African country to establish a national federation. Fourteen federations found the Fédération Internationale de Volleyball (FIVB), with headquarters in Paris.

1948 First European Championship held in Rome and won by Czechoslovakia. Following the end of World War II, the rules are rewritten and clarified to make interpretation easier.

1949 The first Men's World Championship is held in Prague.

1952 The first Women's World Championship is held in Moscow.

1955 Volleyball is put on the programme for the Pan-American Games.

1958 The Czechs introduce a new defensive hit – the bagger – which amazes spectators at the European Championships in Prague.

1964 New rules on blocking: airborne invasion during blocking is prohibited, while blockers are permitted a second hit. The first Olympic Volleyball tournaments are played at the Tokyo Olympic Games.

1965 The first men's World Cup is played in Poland and won by the USSR.

1967 The first African Continental Championship is played.

1972 The official rules of Mini Volleyball are established. The first South American Junior Championships are held in Rio de Janeiro, Brazil.

1973 The first Women's World Cup is played in Uruguay.

1977 The first Junior World Championships are held in Brazil.

1980 The rules of the game are adopted in three languages: French, English and Spanish.

1986 Beach volleyball receives official status by the FIVB.

1988 The FIVB inaugurates its new headquarters in Lausanne, Switzerland.

1989 The birth of the Beach Volleyball World Series.

1990 The first tournament of the men's World League, with US$1 million dollars prize money.

1993 The first Grand Prix, the women's version of the World League, is played in Asia.

1995 Volleyball is 100 years old.

1996 At the Atlanta Olympic Games, beach volleyball becomes an Olympic medal sport.

1998 Further changes to the rules include playing with a coloured ball and the use of a 'libero' player.

2000 Following the phenomenal success of beach volleyball at the Sydney Olympics, the IOC Executive Committee declares beach volleyball an official Olympic sport.

GLOSSARY

Ace A served ball that lands within the playing boundaries, which is untouched or unplayable by the receiving team and scores points.

Attack block A block which sees the players aggressively target the spiked ball by reading the spiker's actions and intentions.

Block An attempt by a player or players to interrupt the ball before, during or just after it crosses the net.

Bump (pass) Technique of playing the ball using forearms, with hands together, to direct the ball.

Carry A fault called if the ball comes to rest in the course of contact by one player.

Contacted ball A contacted ball is one that touches or is touched by any part of a player's body or clothing.

Court The playing surface divided into two equal areas by a net. In its official form, volleyball is played on a rectangular court 18m (59 ft 1 in) long and 9m (29 ft 6 in) wide; the net is placed 2.24m (7 ft 4 in) high.

Coverage Most often refers to backing up a partner's hit when the block is up and the ball comes back.

Cross court/cut shot An offensive hit when a player, instead of hitting with power, slices the ball just over and nearly parallel to the net.

Dig Used to play a ball that is too low to volley; sometimes called a 'forearm pass'.

Dink A very softly hit spike; ball played just over the net.

Double fault When players from opposing teams commit faults simultaneously. In such cases, the referee will direct a replay.

Dump When the setter, instead of setting the ball for the hitters, dinks the ball over the net.

Floater A serve that 'floats' through the air because it has no spin.

Foot fault When a player steps on to the court or out of bounds before serving the ball.

Free ball A ball the opponent cannot attack and must yield by passing over the net.

Joust When two players on opposing sides attempt to block the ball at the same time pushing it onto each other's side of the net.

J-stroke Using a 'bent elbow' passing technique to pull a ball out of the net.

Kill An attack that results in an immediate point or side-out.

Knuckler An emergency one-handed technique used to save balls set tight to the net. The fingers are curled and the ball hits the heel of the hand to be punched up.

Off hand side Right hand player, playing right side. The ball comes across the body on a set to hit.

On hand side Right hand player, playing left side. The ball is in front of a player on a set to hit.

Out of bounds The ball is out of bounds when it touches any surface, object or ground outside the court. Any part of the ball touching a boundary line or inside the poles of the net is not out of bounds. If the ball is caught or is contacted by a player before landing out of bounds, it is not judged as out of bounds.

Pancake A one-handed floor defensive technique. The hand is extended and slid along the floor, palm down, and the ball rebounds off the back of the hand, rather than the floor.

Pass The first of three contacts on the offensive side, overhead or forearm.

Red card A more severe sanction given by the referee.

Roof To block a spike, usually straight down and for one point. Also known as 'putting the clamps on'.

Screening An attempt by a player to conceal the start of a team-mate's serve by obstructing an opponent's line of sight. Screening is illegal.

Seams The space between the blockers and between back-court defenders.

Serve The act of putting the ball into play.

Shank To pass the ball badly.

Side-out Should the team who receives the serve win the rally, a side-out is awarded. The team receives no point, but becomes the serving team for the next play. When rally scoring, the receiving team also receives a point.

Sky ball A serve that is hit very high into the air. Often done to confuse the opponent, especially if conditions are sunny and windy.

Spiked ball Other than a served ball, a ball hit forcibly from a height not less than the top of the net. Also known as a bury, crush, hammer, kill, put-away or slam.

Sprawl The finishing defensive position on a hard spike that could hit in front of the defender.

Tape shot A spike or ball that hits the top of the net and dribbles over.

Target The designated area from where the setter runs the attack.

Tool(ed) To 'wipe off' (see below) a shot of the blocker is 'to tool'. To have a ball wiped off oneself is 'to be tooled'.

Wipe off To hit the ball off the opposing block so it then heads out of bounds.

Yellow card Warning given by the referee.

INDEX